9 x 3/89 2/10 x

14 ≠ 6 - 18
8 - 20

D1505828

KARATE

MARTIAL AND FIGHTING ARTS SERIES

KARATE

NATHAN JOHNSON

**Senior Consultant Editor
Aidan Trimble (6th Dan)**
Former World, European, and
British Karate Champion
Chairman and Chief Instructor to the
Federation of Shotokan Karate

MASON CREST PUBLISHERS
www.masoncrest.com

Mason Crest Publishers Inc.
370 Reed Road
Broomall, PA, 19008
(866) MCP-BOOK (toll free)
www.masoncrest.com

First printing

1 2 3 4 5 6 7 8 9 10

Library of Congress Cataloging-in-Publication Data on file at the Library of Congress

ISBN 1-59084-388-6

Editorial and design by
Amber Books Ltd.
Bradley's Close
74–77 White Lion Street
London N1 9PF
www.amberbooks.co.uk

Project Editor Chris Stone
Design www.stylus-design.com
Picture Research Lisa Wren

Color reproduction by MRM Graphics, England
Printed and bound in Jordan

IMPORTANT NOTICE
The techniques and information described in this publication are for use in dire circumstances only where the safety of the individual is at risk. Accordingly, the publisher and copyright owner cannot accept any responsibility for any prosecution or proceedings brought or instituted against any person or body as a result of the use or misuse of the techniques and information within.

Picture Credits
Paul Clifton: 12, 15, 17, 37, 47, 48, 63, 74, 79, 82, 85.
Nathan Johnson: 8, 18, 25, 32, 35, 42, 45, 46, 50, 51, 58, 60, 65, 66, 73, 77, 87.
Sporting Pictures: 6.

Front cover image: Paul Clifton.

Contents

Introduction

When I began studying the martial arts back in 1972, the whole subject was shrouded in mystery; indeed, that was part of the attraction. At that time there was only a limited range of books on the subject and therefore very little information was available to the novice.

I am glad to say that this has changed in recent years beyond all recognition. With the explosion of interest in the martial arts and the vast array of quality books that are now on the market, we seem to be increasing our knowledge and understanding of the martial arts and sports science, and this fact is reflected in this new series of books.

Over the past 30 years, I have been privileged to compete, train, and teach with practitioners from most of the disciplines covered in this series. I have coached world champions, developed and adapted training methods for people with disabilities, and instructed members of the armed forces in close-quarter techniques. I can warmly recommend this series as a rich source of information for students and instructors alike. Books can never replace a good instructor and club, but the student who does not study when the training is finished will never progress.

Aidan Trimble—Sixth Dan, Former World Karate Champion

When delivering a blow in karate, the maximum effect of the blow can be reached if the whole of your being is put into the blow. In karate, this is achieved by the use of a "spirit-shout," or *kia*.

What Is Karate?

Karate is the Japanese word for a martial art that uses blocking, punching, striking, kicking, seizing, grappling, and throwing techniques. Karate is written using two Japanese characters: "kara," which means empty, and "te," which means hand or hands. Karate, therefore, is "the art of empty hands," or the art of fighting without weapons.

There are two basic approaches to karate. The first is traditional karate, which is studied as a martial art. The second is sport, or competitive, karate. Many karate associations practice and teach both types of approaches.

There are many reasons why **karate-ka** (people who practice karate) choose to do so. Some are interested in learning self-defense, while others practice it as a sport. There are also many people who do it just for fun. A stimulating and absorbing martial art, karate can be practiced in a group, with a friend, or even alone. Karate is suitable for all ages and levels of fitness, and training can be customized to suit all individuals, including people with disabilities. Most karate schools have a progressive curriculum, starting with the most basic techniques and working up to those that require considerable skill.

Practicing karate increases confidence, improves posture, and cultivates power, grace, and skill. Karate also fosters patience, tolerance, and

The ultimate goal in karate is to defeat the enemy without fighting. But if it becomes necessary to fight, a good defense is essential. The woman in this photograph demonstrates a classic blocking technique.

This illustration depicts the Japanese characters (kanji) for "empty hands," meaning karate.

understanding. In fact, the virtues developed through proper karate training often outweigh its combative value; after all, the one thing a well-trained karate-ka wants to avoid is a fight. In this sense, karate really is not about fighting—it is actually about not fighting!

BREAKING TECHNIQUES

Karate was first introduced to the West in the 1960s (Western karate teachers were still learning the art in the 1950s) and was seen as something new and exotic. Often, the highlight of a karate demonstration was the showing of the "breaking techniques," called **tameshiwara**. Some schools still teach these techniques today, where they are part of the grading requirement for a black belt. However, most modern karate schools no longer practice breaking techniques because they can lead to injury.

Originally devised in ancient times as both a test of strength and a means of demonstration, there are, of course, natural limits to what a human can smash or break with bare hands. The typical materials chosen to be broken are softwood squares measuring 12 x 12 in (30 x 30 cm) and

0.5 in (1.25 cm) thick, and small terra-cotta roof tiles. The wood is broken across the grain. Provided it is held securely and hit reasonably hard, several pieces can easily be broken at once. The requirements for smashing an impressive stack of roofing tiles are patience, the knowledge of how to stack them with proper gaps in between, and the confidence to strike them cleanly. In fact, even people with little or no karate training could break these materials using karate techniques if they were shown how to do so.

Wood and tiles are not the only materials used in breaking demonstrations; the types of materials used are limited only by the imaginations of those concerned. Some karate demonstrators have broken stones, chopped the tops off standing beer bottles (not recommended), and dramatically smashed huge blocks of ice. There are even contests in which people compete to see who can break the most items in a given time.

As exciting as it may sound, the ability to break an object using karate techniques contributes nothing to being able to hit a moving target, a much more useful benefit of karate. For the purposes of this book, it is suggested that you do not attempt these techniques, as the only thing you may end up breaking is your arm, hand, or fist.

A BIT OF HISTORY

Karate originated in China, where self-defense methods were popular, particularly during the Ming Dynasty (1368–1644). Gradually, the techniques developed by the Chinese masters—and mistresses, too—spread throughout Asia, eventually finding a home on the Ryukyu Island of Okinawa, one of a small chain of islands roughly midway between China and Japan.

Karate has deep spiritual roots that can be traced back to ancient temples—like the one shown here—places where people still go to train themselves rigorously in martial arts.

By the mid-17th century, a small and elite group of karate-ka secretly molded the Chinese techniques into several versions of their own, which they referred to only as "te," meaning "hand." The three leading schools of the day were located in three major Okinawan cities: Shuri, Naha, and Tomari. Each school had its own distinctive characteristics, which were recorded in choreographed sequences of martial arts movements known as "**kata**."

In 1917, and again in 1922, a group of prominent Okinawan karate masters toured the Japanese mainland to promote karate. Karate quickly became popular, eventually spreading to the U.S., Europe, Australia, and then to most parts of the world. Today, karate is a household word.

KARATE STYLES

There are many different styles, or schools, of karate worldwide, making for a rich tapestry of associations with differing aims, objectives, protocols, and

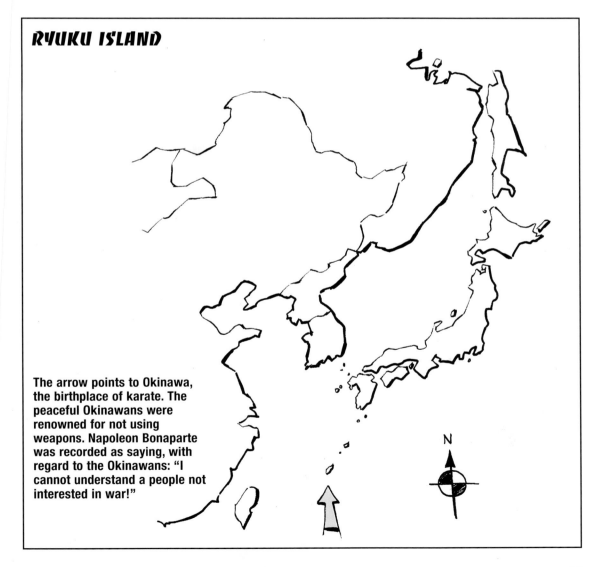

RYUKU ISLAND

The arrow points to Okinawa, the birthplace of karate. The peaceful Okinawans were renowned for not using weapons. Napoleon Bonaparte was recorded as saying, with regard to the Okinawans: "I cannot understand a people not interested in war!"

N

training methods. There are, however, certain core values that most karate teachers and practitioners hold dear. Perhaps one of the most important is that karate should be an art of defense, not offense. This means that karate should not be used to indiscriminately attack others; rather, it should be used for self-improvement and self-defense—and even then only under extreme provocation.

The following are 10 of the most popular and well-known karate styles, practiced throughout the world.

SHOTOKAN

Founders: students of Master Funakoshi (Shoto was Master Funakoshi's pen name).

Description: an eclectic and comprehensive karate style that tends to set the norms and standards that many other styles follow.

GOJU-RYU

Founder: Master Chojun Miyagi.

Description: a powerful Okinawan style of karate that specializes in close-quarter combat. Based largely on Fukien Chinese kung fu.

GOJU KAI

Founder: Master Gogen Yamaguchi (1909–1989). A student of Chojun Miyagi. Master Yamaguchi was also known as "The Cat" and was a famous karate figure. The Emperor of Japan decorated him for his services to karate.

Description: goju kai is a Japanese version of Okinawan goju-ryu.

SHITO-RYU

Founder: Kenwa Mabuni (1889–1957). Shito-ryu is a combination of the two "kanji" (calligraphy characters) of the names of Sensei Mabuni's teachers. Sensei Mabuni was an influential figure in Japanese karate, largely because of his immense knowledge of a variety of karate kata.

Description: shito-ryu is a blend of Naha and Shuri karate—the two fundamental Okinawan karate categories or approaches.

WADO-RYU

Founder: Master Hironori Otsuka (1892–1982). The Emperor decorated Master Otsuka for his services to karate.

Description: this style of karate is characterized by fluid, non-resistive techniques that agree with an attacker's force and direction, seeking

When executing the techniques of karate kata, the eyes move first, followed by the hips, and then the legs—they all arrive together.

to actively make use of both to gain victory. Accordingly, wado-ryu is translated as "the way of harmony, or peace."

WADO-KAI

Founders: students of Master Otsuka (see Wado-ryu). One of the most prominent of these founders is the incredible karate technician, Professor Tatsuo Suzuki, possibly one of the finest modern karate-ka.

Description: similar to wado-ryu (see page 15).

SHORIN-RYU

Founder: based on karate taught by the legendary Sokon "Bushi" (warrior) Matsumura (1796–1893).

Description: a broad-based term for a type of karate from Shuri. A fast, light karate style that was a major influence on the shotokan and wado-ryu styles.

UECHI-RYU

Founder: Master Kanbun Uechi (1877–1948).

Description: a close-quarters system with similarities to goju-ryu. Based largely on the Fukian Chinese kung fu.

SHOTOKAI

Founders: students of Master Funakoshi. One prominent master of shotokai is Britain's Mistsusuke Harada, a **sensei** who was graded to fifth dan directly by Master Funakoshi.

Description: Harada sensei's karate is inspirational, subtle, and deep in spiritual content.

To use a metaphor: merely learning to fight is to treat the symptom. Karate is designed to cure the disease. But this requires strength—of body and mind. Both can be trained through kata. The karate technique shown here is from the goju-ryu kata "superenpai."

There is no karate without courtesy, dignity, self-discipline, and concentration. Here, a young student stands still in an attitude of attention. All students must respect their martial arts teachers.

KYOKUSHINKAI

Founder: Masatatsu Oyama (1923–1994). Some have called Masatatsu Oyama the greatest karate master in the world. He did much to bring the art of karate into the public eye.

Description: perhaps the strongest type of karate, featuring full-contact blows.

THE VALUE OF KARATE

There are many stories about the legendary power that karate masters of old could demonstrate. They trained for countless hours and were invincible warriors. They could beat the bad guys, teach their students, paint beautiful pictures, write excellent poetry, talk on equal terms with the wisest of men and women, and still be home in time for supper. That said, while serious training in karate brings skill and power, with that power comes responsibility—responsibility not to be a show-off or a braggart and not to misuse the skills gained.

The unique power of karate is not found in the efficiency of its techniques alone, but in the incredible fusion of body and mind that the skilled karate-ka can call upon; a fusion of body and mind that leads to the type of skill that past observers thought was mystical. This karate of old, and all it has to offer, is still available to us today. The value of karate can be classified in three ways: as a form of exercise, as a form of self-defense, and as a form of self-discipline and training.

EXERCISE

Karate is interesting as a form of exercise because it can be practiced without equipment, a uniform, or even a partner. Very little space is needed, and techniques can be sharpened, or honed, for as little as a few minutes at a time to as long as an hour or more. Karate is effective as an exercise because it is balanced; its techniques are practiced on both sides of the body, and the body is moved in all directions.

As the accumulated experience of karate practice grows, so does the karate-ka's skill and capacity for exercise, making karate progressive. In this sense, karate today is an interesting challenge. With new things to learn all the time, it has become a passion and a lifetime quest for many thousands of people worldwide.

SELF-DEFENSE

Most living creatures practice some form of self-defense, and this certainly applies to humans, who can perhaps be said to specialize in the use of weapons. The mystical art of karate is, however, special. It uses no weapons other than the trained body of the karate-ka and seeks to rise above animal instinct.

Karate as a form of self-defense has great value if you are prepared to be guided by the wisdom of generations of karate masters and do not seek to misuse karate skills. The attraction of karate as a form of self-defense lies in its reputation as an art that smaller, weaker people can use to great effect against larger, stronger opponents. It is useful to remember, however, that ultimately, in karate, the real opponent is oneself.

SELF-DISCIPLINE

Karate as a form of self-discipline may not sound all that attractive until we realize that discipline leads to efficiency, and that preparation often leads to success. Karate is a structured discipline with efficient techniques. It excels as a method of spiritual training and cultivation because it emphasizes decency, courtesy, humility, and humanity.

GETTING STARTED

We will now take a look at the preparation required to make karate practice safe, enjoyable, and productive.

THE KARATE UNIFORM

Most traditional karate schools encourage students to obtain and wear a uniform often referred to as a gi (pronounced gee). Traditionally, this is a loose-fitting, white, two-piece set consisting of pants and a wrap-around jacket. Less traditional schools use colored uniforms, tracksuits, or even t-shirts. Wearing a gi makes everybody more or less the same. Karate-ka cannot hide behind their everyday image—fashion and expensive clothing are unimportant—and thus group identity and comradeship are fostered.

THE KARATE GI AND BELT

The famous karate gi and obi are based on ancient everyday Chinese clothing. The karate gi is practical, comfortable, and serviceable.

21

THE BOW

Training begins and ends with a bow. This is known as Rei ni hajimari rei ni owaru.

Used only during karate practice, a gi is both comfortable and durable. Students are encouraged to keep their gi clean; to keep finger- and toenails short (or at least trimmed); and to remove (or cover with tape) all jewelry in order to avoid scratching themselves and others.

The gi is tied with a belt or **obi** (pronounced obee) that indicates the rank or grade of the individual. Although ranking systems vary between schools, beginners usually wear a white belt and work their way up to a black belt. A common belt-ranking system uses the following belt colors, in order of beginner to advanced: white, yellow, orange, green, blue, brown, and black. There are further divisions of the black belt, called "dans," meaning levels, with some schools going up to tenth dan. To get to tenth dan often takes a lifetime. In fact, most tenth dans are over 70 years of age! Gichin Funakoshi, one of the founding fathers of modern Japanese karate, was well over 50 when he began his famous "mission" to spread karate throughout Japan.

It takes anywhere from two to five years to reach the rank of black belt, depending on the school, the style or association you belong to, and how often (and hard) you train. It should always be remembered, however, that karate skills themselves are much more important than the uniform or rank, which, after all, are only a means to an end. Training alone in your home, your yard, or the park can be just fine. In fact, some old karate masters used to train in their everyday clothes.

WARM-UP EXERCISES

LEFT: The triceps stretch prepares the upper arm for the rigors of karate training.

BELOW: Stretching and warm-up should start with the most basic and progress to the most difficult. In this example, a leg stretch is combined with a back, shoulder, and arm stretch.

BILL "SUPERFOOT" WALLACE

American karate champ and legend Bill "Superfoot" Wallace had his side kick clocked at a staggering 60 mph (93 km/h). This increase in entertaining kicking techniques is in keeping with the introduction of the modern sport of karate, which has, to some extent, expanded the original purpose of karate to include a sporting or competitive element, particularly for young people.

TRAINING

Karate training can take place wherever there is enough space, but sports halls, gymnasiums, and karate studios are among the most common venues for classes. The traditional name for a place where karate is practiced is the dojo, with **do** meaning "the way" and **jo** meaning "the place." Essentially, dojo means "the place where 'the way' (in this case, karate) is practiced." Other Japanese martial arts also refer to their places of training as a dojo. It is customary to perform a bow of respect upon entering and leaving the dojo and before and after training with a partner. The bow, or "**rei**," is also used before and after performing a kata.

SAFETY

The number one rule in karate training is safety. There is no point in risking, let alone sustaining, an injury during training. That would be counterproductive. Self-defense starts with looking after yourself by preparing properly and training sensibly.

Before starting to train in karate, most karate-ka warm up, gently stretching and exercising the body in order to avoid strains, muscle pulls, and other injuries.

Basic warm-up movements may include the triceps stretch, circling the arms, circling the waist, squatting on the heels, stretching the hamstrings, and sitting with the soles of the feet pressed together and pushing the knees to the floor (which is known as the butterfly). Modern karate training is usually divided into three basic categories.

Karate techniques fuse beauty with function and are therefore both practical and attractive, as we can see in this "adapted" shorin-ryu technique.

SIDE KICK

The side kick is possibly, with the exception of the "turning" or "round" kick, the most popular of karate kicks. It is not, however, the most practical. It works best if it is kept low and if accompanied with strong hand techniques.

KIHON: THE BASICS

The basic movements are considered to be the most important or essential defensive and offensive movements of karate. Karate-ka should practice the basics so thoroughly that they become instinctive.

Shoshine Nagamine, an Okinawan karate great, informs us that, "Only long and extensive training through repetition will enable the student to fuse all of his strength into the movements of kata. Generations of experience have shown that it usually requires three years to learn the basics and seven years to acquire a fundamental proficiency of kata. Practice of the basic movements enables the student to achieve a natural, beautiful, swift, stable, and powerful performance of kata. From this come the reflexes and spontaneous movements necessary for defense and offense in actual combat. Thus, mastery of karate-do begins with the basic movements."

KATA: SOLO CHOREOGRAPHED KARATE SEQUENCES

There is a large number of karate kata, both ancient and modern. Some schools practice only three, while others practice as many as 50. Master Funakoshi said that a truly great karate expert would not know more than five kata. That was said a long time ago, however, and today, most schools teach between 8 and 30 kata. Some modern karate styles do not practice kata at all, preferring instead to concentrate on sports, free-fighting competitions, or less traditional methods of self-defense.

According to the karate expert and historian Patrick McCarthy, "By learning kata, students of karate walk in the footsteps of the greatest karate experts who have ever lived." He goes on to list some of the physical aims of kata practice as strengthening bone and muscle and developing fast reflexes and movements.

There are also nonphysical aims of kata training, including the production of a state of mind that balances confidence with humility and focuses concentration through alertness.

Every movement or technique in a kata has both a function and a purpose. There are no movements just for show (unlike karate movies or computer games), and each kata has its own special technique. Once the solo movements of a given kata have been thoroughly learned, the karate-ka begins to practice the applications with or against another person. The practical application of karate kata is often called **bunkai**.

KUMITE: SPARRING

Sparring, unlike the fixed applications of formal kata, consists of a fluid exchange of techniques between two people. Karate sparring is a new

STANCES

STANCE 1: Front-leg-bent stance (zenkutsu-dachi). One of karate's most used and general stances.

STANCE 2: Back-leg-bent stance (kokutsu-dachi). This stance is used mostly in traditional karate.

STANCE 3: Cat stance (nekoashi-dachi). This stance, along with the sachin stance, is favored by goju-ryu karate.

addition to karate, and most sparring tactics and the rules for karate competitions or tournaments were only worked out in the 1940s and 1950s. Most of the masters of old did not engage in sparring at all, preferring instead to stick to kata practice. Interestingly, as sparring has developed, it has come to include more and more spectacular kicking techniques—particularly high ones—and most competition fighters have their own crowd-pleasing techniques.

STANCE

Posture, or stance, is fundamental to all three categories of karate training. Karate stances should provide stability and balance for blocking, punching, striking, kicking, and grappling or locking, while also allowing for flexibility and mobility. Let us now take a look at some of the most important and well-used karate stances.

NATURAL, OR READY, STANCE (SHIZENTAI-DACHI)

Stand with your feet a little more than shoulder-width apart. Relax your shoulders, and hold your clenched fists in front of and away from your body. Keep the elbows slightly bent (some schools prefer to straighten the arms fully).

FRONT-LEG-BENT STANCE (ZENKUTSU-DACHI)

Stretch your back leg behind you completely straight (or nearly straight, as in some schools). Bend your front leg until your knee makes a vertical line with your toes. Keep your hips balanced. This is a strong stance for both offense and defense.

BACK-LEG-BENT STANCE (KOKUTSU-DACHI)

Extend your front leg and bend your rear leg, supporting about 70 percent of your weight on it. This stance is primarily used for defense.

CAT STANCE (NEKOASHI-DACHI)

The cat stance is a narrower version of the back-leg-bent stance. Stand with your back leg bent and supporting about 90 percent of your weight. Hover your front leg so that only the ball of your foot touches the ground. Unlike the back-leg-bent stance, the cat stance is not necessarily used only for defensive purposes. Often, the cat stance is used to position the karate-ka alongside an attacking opponent.

THREE-CONFLICTS STANCE (SANCHIN-DACHI)

Stand with your feet approximately one-and-a-half shoulder widths apart. Bend your knees, and turn your feet in. Grip the ground with your feet, and let your hips fall into a natural position. Keep your shoulders down and square. This is a good stance to use when engaged in seizing and grappling techniques, as it is strong against both pushes and pulls.

FORMING A PROPER KARATE FIST

Clenching the fist properly has always been considered important by karate masters. It is a good habit to get into right from the start. Traditionally, the clenched fist is called seiken. To make it, bend the fingers at the second joint, clench them tightly into the palm, and press both the forefinger and the middle finger together with the thumb. Keep the wrist flat and level with the top of the forearm.

MAKING A FIST

STEP 1: Straighten the hand.

STEP 2: Raise the thumb while simultaneously curling the fingers tightly.

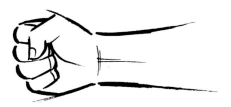

STEP 3: Pay particular attention to tightening the little, index, and middle fingers and press the thumb tightly into the index and middle fingers.

STEP 4: Try hard to reduce the "angle" of the fist to 90 degrees or less and keep the back of the wrist straight.

STEP 5: The parts of the fist that actually land are the first two knuckles, the index and middle finger knuckles, which are referred to as "kento," or fist sword.

There is No First Attack in Karate

Although karate-ka practice offensive, or attacking, techniques, karate is primarily an art of defense. As such, in traditional karate, the first move must be a defensive one; only then can an offensive move, or counterattack, be made.

This is best explained by the phrase, "There is no first attack in karate" (karate nisente-nashi), which is fundamental to the art and a mantra of those that study karate. Naturally, the blocking techniques of karate were developed with this in mind.

These techniques fall into two broad categories: those performed with the clenched fist, and those performed with the open hand. Karate blocking techniques, like other karate techniques, are performed at three heights: upper (**jodan**, pronounced joe-dan), middle (**chudan**, pronounced choo-dan), and lower (**gedan**, pronounced gai-dan). Blocks are referred to as uke (pronounced ookay), but to translate uke as "block" is not entirely accurate, as uke actually means "to receive." A better way to think of karate blocks might be to think of them as ways to intercept an attack by using force to unbalance the attacker before counterattacking.

The soft can overcome the hard—the weak can overcome the strong. Skillful use of karate techniques allows the weaker player to overcome the stronger, as illustrated in this knife-hand block.

BODY EVASION

There is a saying in karate: "Avoid rather than block. Block (check) rather than strike." The best defense is, of course, to not be in the place of danger in the first place. In karate, the next best defense is to avoid an attack by repositioning. The karate term used to describe repositioning, or body shifting, is **tenshin.**

The most obvious method of tenshin is to run away, although technically speaking, this is not really tenshin. Unfortunately, due to some rather suspect—not to mention misguided—notions of heroism, running away is sorely underrated these days. After all, where would we be if our karate heroes ran away? We would not have any entertainment in karate fight scenes for a start, because the karate-ka would be too well trained in running! In our society, the act of running away tends to be thought of in negative terms, as though it is a cowardly act. But running away is not always the action of a coward—even the most ferocious animals are good at running away when the need arises. Indeed, running away is one of nature's primary and most useful instincts.

Of course, there are times when we cannot run away, for whatever reason, and must therefore take action. When running away is not an option and we are forced to defend ourselves, in karate, we turn to tenshin, or body evasion. Tenshin can best be understood or described in terms of the points of the compass. There are four basic directions that can be taken, and eight in all, depending on whether you move left or right.

FORWARD

Going forward into an attack can be a form of evasion in that an attack can

"What is more yielding than water? Yet what can overcome it?" This is the kind of thinking that has led to karate's fluid evasion techniques, an example of which is shown here. The player in the foreground moves to the left to avoid his opponent's kick.

be thwarted, stifled, muffled, and spoiled. "Be as a dragonfly that perches on (the back of) a stick raised to hit it" is one quote that springs to mind.

BACKWARDS

Moving backwards is natural and easy. However, it can be dangerous, as your opponent can continue moving forward and may move faster than you can move backwards.

SIDEWAYS AND BACKWARDS

Moving sideways and backwards can be effective because it forces your opponent to readjust in order to follow you.

SIDEWAYS AND FORWARDS

Moving sideways and forwards can also be effective, provided that you have good close-quarters skills and can neutralize any attacks directed at you. Karate joint-locking techniques work well at this close range.

DISTANCE

A proper understanding of **maai**, or relative distance, is vital when using tenshin. If your opponent is out of range, you can keep him or her continually out of distance by skillful control of the maai (the Shotokai style of karate specializes in this). The natural distance to take from an opponent is approximately the length of your own leg.

When you are in a state of alert, anyone that enters within your natural maai will trigger your body into the fight-or-flight mode. You can discover just how true this is by trying the following simple experiment. Stand in a natural ready stance (shizentai-dachi), and have a friend stand about 10 paces away from you. Ask your friend to begin to walk slowly towards you while looking into your eyes. Stand still and, relying on your natural instincts, shout "Stop!" in a loud voice at the very moment when you feel threatened. When you say stop, your friend should do so instantly.

It might take you a few tries to get it right, but when you do, you will notice that you have halted your friend at the precise point at which he or

There are three main hindrances to success in karate: kiki oji, fear of the enemy's reputation; mikuzure, fear of the enemy's appearance; and futanren, inadequate training. Only hard and proper training can overcome these obstacles.

BLOCKS

LOWER BLOCK: Step forward and block strongly, keeping your hips balanced and your back straight.

MIDDLE BLOCK: When blocking at middle level, make sure that your body remains at the same height while you are stepping forward.

UPPER BLOCK: To block effectively at the upper level, keep the shoulders down and keep the blocking arm relaxed until the moment of impact.

she was about to break into your personal space, or maai, and at a distance where he or she cannot reach you with a punch or kick.

Staring into your friend's eyes at your natural maai is easy enough. But now, ask your friend to continue to stare into your eyes and to slowly move closer into your maai. You will notice a feeling of intimidation as the person moves closer to you.

In karate, the rule for controlling what happens with regards to maai is simple: keep strict control of your own maai. If your maai is entered by an opponent, you must already be engaged in the actions of defending and counterattacking, or you must be controlling and immobilizing the limbs of your opponent.

BLOCKING TECHNIQUES

Blocking techniques, the cornerstone of karate, are executed in conjunction with both tenshin and maai.

When using blocking techniques, it is important not to overblock or block too far away from the body, or you will be vulnerable to another attack. Keep your shoulders down and finish the blocking technique in the proper position.

LOWER BLOCK (GEDAN UKE)

The lower block is performed by sweeping down and forward with the blocking arm, starting from a position where the arm is raised near the shoulder of your opposite arm. The clenched fist of the blocking arm is rotated so that the palm faces the neck and is then rotated to be palm-down at the completion of the block.

MIDDLE BLOCK (CHUDAN UDE-UKE)

The middle block is performed by crossing the blocking arm, clenched fists palm-down, under the supporting arm, and then sweeping out and forward. Rotate the fist of the blocking arm to be palm-up at the completion of the block. This block is usually performed at the height of your shoulder, although some schools use it as an upper-level block.

UPPER BLOCK (JODAN UDE-UKE)

The upper block is performed by crossing the blocking arm, clenched fists palm-up, under the supporting arm, and then sweeping up and forward. Rotate the fist of the blocking arm to be palm-forward at the completion of the block. This block is usually performed at head height.

OPEN-HAND BLOCK

Open-hand blocking techniques are mostly performed with the hand stretched and straightened into a knife-hand position. To make the knife-hand position, join the four fingers of the hand you are using and press the thumb (bent at the first joint) to the root of your forefinger.

KNIFE-HAND POSITION

The little-finger edge of the outstretched hand is the anatomical weapon used in the famous "karate chop." Used properly, it can produce devastating results.

KNIFE-HAND BLOCK (CHUDAN SHUTO-UKE)

Prepare to perform this block in a similar fashion as the lower block, only this time, open both of your hands to form knife-hands. Sweep the blocking hand forward and out in an arc, rotating the palm of your blocking hand to block with the knife-hand at the level of your shoulder. As with the middle block, this block can also be used as an upper block.

PUNCHING AND STRIKING TECHNIQUES (TSUKI AND UCHI)

Traditionally, punching and striking techniques are treated separately in the classification of karate techniques. However, in this book, they will be considered together.

THE KARATE "SPIRIT-SHOUT," OR KIA

When delivering a blow in karate, the maximum effect of the blow can be reached if the whole of your being is put into the blow. In karate, this is achieved by the use of a "spirit-shout," or kia. In the same way that a weightlifter lets out a deep and audible grunt when lifting a heavy weight, or a boxer exhales forcefully when punching, a karate-ka harnesses the entire force of mind, body, and spirit in a shout intended to maximize the effect of a particular punch, strike, or kick. There is no special sound to make; more important than the actual sound is where it comes from. To be effective, a primal shout must be generated deep in the belly, rumble irresistibly upward, be formulated in the throat, burst out loudly, and frighten the heck out of an opponent. The kia is most frequently used in combination with the reverse- or rear-hand punch (see page 43). There are three basic types of punches in karate.

The student in this picture performs a well-executed reverse punch. Champion martial artist, Jo Lewis, revolutionized the karate reverse punch by raising the free hand to protect the head and allowing the rear heel off the ground, thus adding more power to the punch.

FRONT-HAND JAB PUNCH (KAZAMA-TSUKI)

Stand in a front-leg-bent stance. Slide forward by pushing off your back leg and adjusting the front one. Punch forward with your lead hand, taking care to keep the elbow of the punching hand in and down during the punch. Rotate the fist of the punching hand in a "corkscrew" action. Complete the punch with the clenched fist facing palm-down.

FULL-STEPPING PUNCH (OI-TSUKI)

Stand in a front-leg-bent stance. Take one smooth full step forward into a front-leg-bent stance with your opposite leg forward. On completion of the step, "fire" a punch forward, taking care to keep the shoulder of the punching arm well down. Rotate the fist of your punching hand in a corkscrew action. Complete the punch with the clenched fist facing palm-down.

REVERSE- OR REAR-HAND PUNCH (GYAKU-TSUKI)

Stand in a front-leg-bent stance. Before you execute the punch, the hip of your

JAB PUNCH

A good jab punch moves faster than the eye can see. Be ready to follow up with another technique when or after using a jab.

rear leg should be further back than the front hip, giving your profile a characteristic half-facing appearance. This is called **hanmi** in Japanese. The hip is kept back so that when the reverse punch ("reverse" meaning that the opposite hand from the forward leg is being used) is thrown, the twisting action of the hips will add maximum power to the punch. In karate, this is called "putting in the hip," or **koshi o ireru**.

STEPPING PUNCH

STEP 1: Step strongly forward from the front-leg-bent position.

STEP 2: When the stepping foot is firmly placed in a front-leg-bent stance, punch forward, taking care not to raise the shoulders.

In this photograph, the defender has—almost miraculously—avoided a jab punch, but he must be alert to a follow-up technique, most likely a kick. Karate players require exceptional balance to be able to maneuver their way out of the range of an oncoming attack.

BACKFIST STRIKE (URAKEN UCHI)

Stand in a front-leg-bent stance. Raise the striking arm, and aim the blow by lining up the elbow of the striking hand with the intended target. Execute the backfist strike by extending the arm in an arc, and then snapping the blow speedily towards the target in a way similar to flicking out a

Above and opposite: The knife-hand strike has many variations that include the chest knife-hand strike, the double-knife hand strike—aimed at the collarbone—and the supported knife-hand strike, used to attack the ribs.

wet hand-towel. Keep the shoulders down and the striking arm relaxed, and be sure to retract the arm as quickly as you extended it.

KNIFE-HAND STRIKE (SHUTO UCHI)

There are various ways of delivering knife-hand strikes, but the most common is the well-known "karate chop." Stand in a back-leg-bent stance. Raise the striking hand (palm forward) above your head. Pay particular attention to forming the knife-hand position properly, and keep the thumb of the striking hand well tucked in to avoid injury. Shifting your weight forward and moving from the back-leg-bent stance to the front-leg-bent stance, strike outwards and downwards in a semicircular arc, finishing the blow abruptly at shoulder height and in the midline of your body.

Karate Kicking Techniques

We have now reached the part of the book that describes the most dramatic—and often the most popular—techniques in karate: the kicking techniques. Interestingly, the word "karate" means empty hands—and does not even mention feet!

Close examination of the authentic or traditional karate kata reveals that there are very few kicks at all; most techniques are performed using the hands. Modern karate is different, however. It has lots of kicks, which makes for spectacular karate. Because the legs are so much stronger than the arms, kicking techniques, while slower than hand techniques, can be more powerful.

Kicks are best directed at low targets, including the sides of the trunk and the solar plexus. The kicking leg should be pulled back as soon as possible to minimize the vulnerability of being on one leg. Indeed, there is a famous saying in karate: "The trick with the kick is to keep it low, thrust it out, fast-not slow." Although high kicks might be fun to do and may score points in competition, Master Nagamine (a famous Okanawan karate master) advises us that, "To obviate the danger of being tripped, the kicking techniques

The advantage of kicking techniques is that players have a longer reach in which to strike their opponent. The disadvantage with a long reach, however, such as that achieved with this high side kick, is that it gives your opponent a split second longer to stage a counterattack.

must only be used when the opponent is close enough or when caught by the hand or arm." This is definitely something we see mirrored in traditional Southern Chinese kung fu, in which kicks are kept to an absolute minimum. When they are used, it is mostly in conjunction with a hand technique, a lock or trap, an arm bar, or as a diversion.

The high side kick is relatively modern. Senior karate-ka returning to Japan after World War II were shocked to find it being practiced and would not accept it.

Karate history has records of actual encounters or combat incidents using kicks. The following story is about the karate master Chotoku Kyan (1870–1945) and how he defeated an opponent using a kick. When Kyan was 40, a young and powerful bully named Matsuda came to his attention. Matsuda had the unpleasant habit of picking on the youngsters in the village. Kyan went to find the bully, intending to have a few words with him. But when Kyan approached him, Matsuda became aggressive with Kyan. Kyan was a small man (around five feet tall), but he had studied and mastered those secrets of karate that allow a small man to triumph over

The more-traditional low side kick is strong, fast, and capable of fracturing a femur (thighbone) if delivered with enough force.

a larger one. According to Shoshine Nagamine, "The secret is that when a small man faces an opponent, he must not take backwards steps to evade blows or kicks; instead, he should take forward steps or side steps so that he can take the offensive right after defending himself." Indeed, Kyan had trained with his back to a river in order to acquire the habit of going forward.

Matsuda then challenged Kyan to a fight, claiming that even if Kyan were a karate master, he would be nothing in a real fight. Kyan agreed to fight Matsuda and suggested that the fight take place in an empty space near the Hija River. Kyan chose this location wisely, for he had selected the very spot in which he had often trained. With his back to the river, he waited for Matsuda's attack.

Matsuda aimed a blow at Kyan, who instantly shifted his position sideways, escaped the attack, and then kicked Matsuda hard on the outside of the thigh. Matsuda twisted and, spiraling out of control, crashed straight into the river. He came out of the river with a much better attitude and gave up being a bully.

THE FRONT KICK (MAE-GERI)

The front kick is easily the most manageable kick in karate. It is a popular kick that can be well executed by most people who try.

Stand in a front-leg-bent stance. Raise the knee of your kicking leg so that it is at least parallel with the floor. Make sure that the knee of the supporting, or platform, leg is well bent and that the supporting foot is pointing forward. Thrust the kicking leg out and forward while pushing the ankle forward and pulling the toes back, so that if the kick were to land, it

FRONT KICK

STEP 1: Make sure you are relaxed to avoid "telegraphing" (letting your opponent see the kick coming).

STEP 2: Aim the kick by pointing the knee at the target.

STEP 3: "Flick" the kick to the target, taking care not to overextend your knee.

SIDE KICK

STEP 1: Prepare the kick strongly. Standing in the front-leg-bent stance, raise your knee.

STEP 2: Thrust the kick out to the side, making sure you do not bend your head forward, otherwise any impact might unbalance you.

would make contact with the ball of the foot. Some schools of karate make contact using the tips of the toes (ouch!).

THE SIDE KICK (YOKO-GERI)

Stand in the front-leg-bent stance. Raise the knee of your kicking leg so that it is at least parallel with the floor. Make sure that the knee of the supporting, or platform, leg is well bent and that the supporting foot is pointing sideways. Turn the hips until the thigh of the kicking leg faces the intended target and the lead hip is in a comfortable position. Thrust the kicking leg sideways and out while bending the ankle and pulling the toes back. The point of contact is the edge of the foot.

THE ROUND KICK (MAWASHI-GERI)

Stand in the front-leg-bent stance. Raise the knee of your kicking leg so that it is at least parallel with the floor. Make sure that the knee of the supporting, or platform, leg is well bent and that the supporting foot is pointing sideways. Begin to turn the hip of the kicking leg as you flick the leg out in a semicircle. The point of contact should be the top of the arch or the ball of the foot.

ROUND KICK

STEP 1: Ensure that the toes of the supporting leg are turned out and away from the target.

STEP 2: Make sure that you kick only when the hip of the kicking leg is in a safe position.

THE BACK KICK (USHIRO-GERI)

Stand in the front-leg-bent stance. Pivoting on the ball of your front leg, turn your body 180 degrees. Raise the knee of your kicking leg so that it is at least parallel with the floor. Make sure that the knee of the supporting, or platform, leg is well bent and that the supporting foot is pointing directly backwards. Thrust the kicking leg out backwards towards the target. The point of contact should be the heel.

THE JUMPING KICK (TOBI-GERI)

Stand in the front-leg-bent stance. Raise the knee of the rear leg so that the

BACK KICK

STEP 1: Turn to face the target quickly but comfortably. Do not strain turning your head.

STEP 2: Kick outwards and backwards as effortlessly as possible. Turn to face your target as soon as the kick is completed.

JUMPING KICK

STEP 1: Launch yourself strongly into the air, within kicking range of your opponent.

STEP 2: Extend the kick quickly. Take care to keep your back straight so that you can land safely.

thigh is parallel with the floor. Spring off the ground with the front leg; flick out a real or fake front kick with the rear leg, followed swiftly by a mid-air front kick using the front leg.

There are other kicks in the repertoire of modern karate. These include the spinning kick, the flying side kick, the flying round kick, and the jumping-back-spinning kick. These kicks do not appear in traditional kata and are largely modern inventions. There is also a strange kick called the half-crescent kick (mikazuki geri) in which the karate-ka arcs his or her kicking leg in a crescent movement, finishing the technique by slapping the sole of the kicking foot into the palm of the (opposite) outstretched hand. This technique is usually considered to be a blocking technique that makes use of the foot.

SAFETY

When dealing with karate kicking techniques, it is useful to remember that we all have different bodies; or more precisely, that some people are naturally more flexible than others. This means that less-flexible people risk injury if they try to strain their bodies when kicking. The golden rule to observe is to keep kicks as safe and as natural as possible. Unlike most other forms of exercise, in karate we cannot "warm up," stretch, or prepare before using kicks in a self-defense situation. Therefore, it helps to pay par-

Tobi yoko geri is the famous flying side kick. From a safety point of view, the flying side kick is one of the most dangerous—you must give consideration to how you land.

ticular attention to the knee and hip positions during the initial and preparatory stages of a kick, particularly when executing side and round kicks.

The most effective kicks are those that are kept within the individual's natural range of movement. Of course, this range of movement can be successfully extended. However, if it is overextended, damage, or even serious injury (such as groin strain or a hernia), can result. Besides, when it comes to reaching high targets, the hands are best, just as the feet reach lower targets best. And always remember that anyone who injures himself or herself showing off has left the path to wisdom—if he or she was ever on it to begin with.

USING A KICK-BAG

Karate-ka often sharpen kicking skills using a hanging bag. There are many types of bags available for this purpose. The choice of which one to use is typically up to the user, although if you join a karate club, the karate teacher will often specify which type to use. It is important that the bag is not so hard as to cause bruising or damage. It is also important that the bag be properly secured. The kick-bag must also be in good condition to avoid cuts.

Make sure that you are properly warmed up before attempting to use a kick-bag. Standing in the appropriate preparatory position for the kick being used, land the first few kicks lightly, paying particular attention to accuracy. Gradually increase the power and focus of the kicks until you have reached optimum level. It is always advisable to stretch out a little and to "cool down" after using the bag.

Karate Joint-Locking Techniques

Although karate is best known for its blocks, punches, strikes, and kicks, it also has within its kata a full range of restraining, or joint-locking, techniques. These movements include wrist locks, arm locks, and throwing and tumbling techniques, all of which are designed to restrain an opponent.

Gichin Funakoshi (the founding father of Japanese karate) tells an interesting story about one of his karate teachers, Master Yasutsune Itosu. This story can be found in Master Funakoshi's book, *Karate Do Nyumon: The Master Introductory Text*. One night, Master Yasutsune Itosu was visiting the Tsuji district in Naha City, in Okinawa, Japan. He was just about to enter a restaurant when a young man jumped out from the shadows and, yelling a kia, aimed a blow at him. The blow bounced off Itosu's body, and he grabbed the wrist of his attacker. The young man feared his bones would be crushed, so powerful was the grip of the old Master. Itosu did not even turn to look at his attacker; he merely dragged him into the restaurant. Without relaxing his grip on the attacker, Itosu sat down and asked a waitress to bring food and sake (rice wine). When

It has been claimed that an incredible 80 percent of karate kata techniques are for joint-locking. Joint-locking techniques are ideal for restraining an opponent and can lead to rapid submissions.

the wine was brought to the table, Itosu reached for a cup with one hand and dragged his trembling captive around with the other before releasing him and offering him a drink. The young man bowed in deep embarrassment, shame, and awe.

Joint-locking techniques, called kansetsa waza, are interesting because they allow the karate-ka to control opponents instead of punching, striking, or kicking them. This is desirable from a moral point of view because, in theory at least, a karate-ka can defeat opponents without really hurting them. In this respect, joint locking is best seen as a way to restrain a person. This technique can be quite useful for security professionals and law enforcement officers.

THE OLD KARATE

Karate masters of old did not use the kind of karate we have come to know and expect today. Two of the great (if perhaps old-fashioned) concepts behind karate were dignity and nobility. Keeping the back straight; maintaining a proper posture; using special breathing techniques; and making slow, measured movements, as well as fast ones, all contributed to the mystery and beauty of the old karate kata.

The ancient karate restraining techniques originated in China in a branch of kung fu called **Chi-na**, meaning "to seize and grapple (or struggle)." The old, or "antique," kata are packed with good examples of these restraining techniques.

Karate masters of old were often well-respected members of society who spent a lifetime cultivating "the way" of karate, referred to as **karate-do**. However, when people start out in their training, they are often more

The incredible Steve Arneil, the Kyokushinkai knockdown fighter. Steve is a survivor of the 100-man "kumite" (continuous full-contact fights with 100 opponents—without getting knocked out).

interested in the mechanics and techniques of karate, referred to as **karate-jutsu.**

To this day, teachers and writers argue over the differences between karate-do and karate-jutsu. Some hold the extreme view that karate was designed to kill, and only to kill; for instance, to kill an enemy on the battlefield when one had lost one's weapons or had somehow become disarmed. Others hold the opposite extreme view that karate was originally a quaint and well-mannered Oriental ritualized martial arts dance, and that karate techniques have little value in today's tough urban environments.

Some believe that the answer can be found in what will be called here the "fabric of karate." The fabric of karate definitely exists, and people will weave it into the clothes they want to wear. For example, a young person looking for a way to avoid being bullied has a different objective than someone who has already established a fine reputation of, say, successfully coaching several hundred people to black belt, raising money for charity through karate demonstrations, and things of that nature.

A clue to the final answer to the "**jutsu**" versus "do" question can also be found by practicing the old kata. These kata emphasize the cultivation of dignity. They can also improve one's health and increase one's confidence and bearing, all the while never losing sight of how to skillfully and practically control a situation or an opponent.

The exploits of the fictional kung fu Master Li in the karate book *Barefoot Zen* might help here (remember that kung fu was the parent of karate):

In a small village in Southern China, an old man named Li made his way slowly to a tearoom. There was a public festival, and the place was very busy.

Karate combines grace with power. Here, a young karate-ka practices her technique using a focus of concentration known as Zanshin (remaining mind—mental alertness).

Noisy patrons were doing their best to attract the attention of the staff. Taking his time, Li climbed the stairs to the first floor and, fortunately, found himself a small table in a corner of the room.

Amidst the audible hum of the tearoom conversations, the old man became aware of a group of youths who pointed to him before swaggering over.

Eizo Shimabukuru, a tenth dan Okinawan karate master, once claimed that karate techniques consist largely of striking and (joint) locking techniques (not kicking and blocking). Joint-locking techniques were certainly prominent in old-style karate.

"Hey," said one of them. "Aren't you Yao Li, the kung fu man?" The old man felt like cursing his heritage, all the way back to monk Yao, the Shaolin monk who was his ancestor. If people thought you could fight, your reputation would always provoke envy, fear, or even challenges—yes, even for an old man.

Li shook his head negatively, but the youths came and sat near him anyway. At that point, the tea he had ordered arrived. One of the youths insisted on pouring it and began to do so. However, when the cup was full, the youth continued to pour so that the tea spilled over onto the table. Li raised his hand to stem the unnecessary flow, and the youth, who had bargained on this, became aggressive and lashed out at the old man. The blow did not seem to connect squarely, however. Recoiling, the youth tried again.

STRUCTURE OF THE WRIST

The wrist joint is a delicate joint, and so wrist-lock techniques should be practiced with great care. The wrist is made up of eight small bones called the metacarpels. They are joined together by cartilage. One of the metacarpels is called the scaphoid.

It is notoriously weak and prone to fracture and injury, so do not jam or force the locks on, or you may damage someone's wrist. Please experiment slowly, and take care.

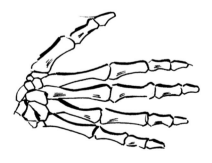

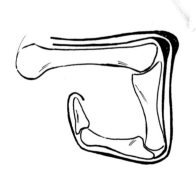

The old man rolled with a practiced ease. Keeping calm, he felt no malice for the youth, only disappointment at the reluctance of others to restrain the offender. Rolling his body with the blows while tangling and trapping the youth's limbs, old man Li didn't counter once. In sheer frustration, the youth redoubled his efforts. Seeking to grab the old man and force him down by sheer strength, he lost his balance when the old man's momentary resistance gave way and coincided with the direction of his own force.

The youth went crashing out of control and into a nearby wall. Such was the force of his attack that the momentum didn't stop there; he bounced off the wall, flipped over, and hit the floor hard. The other youths did not join in.

The youth's next memory was of old man Li bending over him and tending to his injuries. That day, he was educated and, despite his poor

WRIST LOCK

The wrist lock uses a grip known as the "scabbard grip"—a grip technique in which the fingers of your gripping hand point in the same direction as the fingers of your opponent's hand (as shown).

attitude and ill-advised behavior, he was wise enough to understand the lesson. In fact, he became the only student Yao Li would ever take.

What is interesting about this story is that Master Li simply controlled the violence of the hotheaded youth and turned his own strength back upon him. Wrist and arm locks are practical ways of doing precisely that.

WRIST LOCK

An opponent grabs your right wrist. Raise your right arm so that it is vertical and so that your right fist is level with your right shoulder. Open your hand so that your fingers wrap under the gripping wrist and your thumb is posi-

ELBOW LOCK

The elbow lock uses a grip known as the "(sword) handle grip"—a grip technique in which the fingers of your gripping hand point in the opposite direction of your opponent's hand.

tioned on the back of the gripping hand. Grip tightly and, raising your elbow, place your arm so that your elbow is almost parallel with the floor and is slightly higher than your wrist. You may also grip your opponent's fingers with your free hand as you push your opponent's wrist down and to your left (this is called "levering").

DOUBLE LOCK

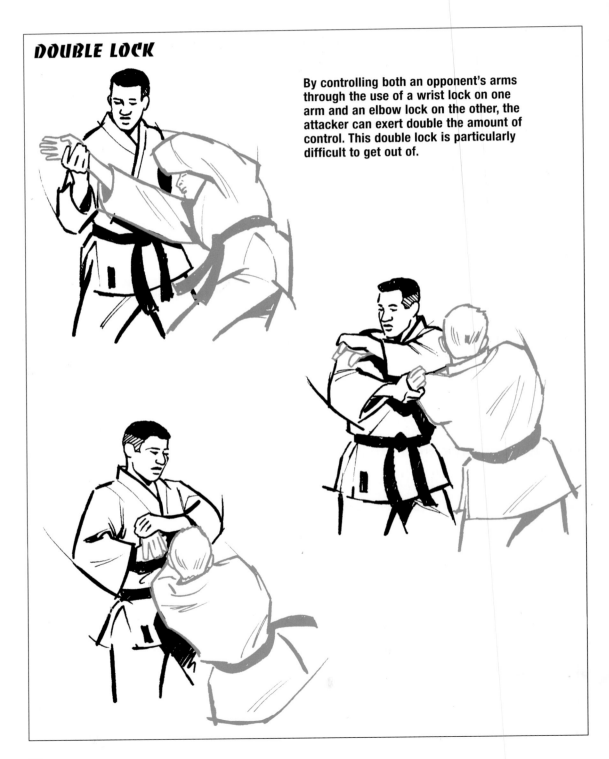

By controlling both an opponent's arms through the use of a wrist lock on one arm and an elbow lock on the other, the attacker can exert double the amount of control. This double lock is particularly difficult to get out of.

MOTOBU RYU

There is a style of karate in Okinawa called motobu ryu that consists almost entirely of locking and throwing techniques. Another style of karate, called zenshorindo, consists almost entirely of grip-release and restraining techniques.

ELBOW LOCK

An opponent grabs your right wrist. Raise your right arm so that it is vertical and so that your right fist is level with your right shoulder. Open your hand and rotate it counterclockwise. Tense your little finger, keep your elbow in and down, and wedge your knife hand into your opponent's wrist to break the grip. Seize your opponent's wrist by gripping on or near the wrist joint and the back of the hand, and then twist your gripping hand in a clockwise circle as you pull your hand towards the side of your body.

DOUBLE-ARM LOCK

The double-arm lock is really a combination of the elbow and wrist locks, and the mechanics are identical.

CLOSING THE DISTANCE TO APPLY LOCKING TECHNIQUES

As we have seen, the act of going forward into an attack can become a form of defense, so long as the attack is neutralized in the process. There is no point in moving towards an attack without the necessary skills to disrupt and neutralize it. Only when you have done that can you seize your opponent's arms prior to beginning the process of locking one or more joints. Of course, this is easier said than done. The problem is that your opponent may well attempt to punch, strike, kick, grapple, or otherwise engage you as you move in.

From a joint-locking and restraining perspective, the key to dealing with any offensive technique is to "cover up" on the way in. This means that you must protect your head and trunk from being hit as you move forward; you must also crowd your opponent. Seek to grab and control one or both arms as you place one of your legs close to your opponent's front leg; by doing this, you can jam any kick that might come your way. This is a positive strategy that takes lots of practice, but is quite effective. You will have to work hard to get it right. The value of this technique lies in the fact that your opponent, who may be unprepared for such an action, will not usually expect it.

GRAPPLING

Grappling is a skill often neglected and misrepresented in karate. After all, karate has become the most well known of the martial arts for its kicks, stances, and acrobatic displays. However, if you imagine the art of grappling to be a noble pursuit in which people can exchange locks and holds in a game (almost like old-fashioned wrestling) and still remain friends after a strenuous bout, I think you will have gained an understanding of the "Old Karate'" contained in the kata.

This joint-locking technique is drawn from the long-lost applications of tekki shodan kata (aka naihanchi and naifuanchin), a kata practiced by several million people, but misunderstood for many years.

Sports and Modern Karate

Competitive karate is a modern phenomenon, yet the urge to compete has long been a human trait. For millennia, humankind has felt the need to challenge any climate it finds itself in and to conquer and master any terrain. Both wild animals and human beings have, at certain times, been viewed as potential opponents in many kinds of struggles.

As human beings, we tend to hold life as being important, particularly our own. From this point of view, self-defense in general—and winning in particular—can be seen as natural human traits.

"The best thing about winning is…winning!" This statement has a certain appeal—no one likes to lose. That said, when two or more people compete, someone must win and someone must lose. Some karate teachers say this reflects the fact that karate is about a win-or-lose (self-defense) situation. Other karate teachers say that karate is not a sport at all. Regardless of one's opinion on the subject, the fact is that although karate was not originally meant to be practiced as a sport, nowadays it has become one. It is the responsibility of all karate-ka to ensure that traditional karate does not decline as a result of the introduction of sports karate.

Karate contests are—on the whole—safer than any other contact sports, and injury rates are relatively low. By learning the art at an established school you will learn the safest way to execute winning moves.

KARATE CODE OF CONDUCT

There is an old saying that sums up the correct karate-ka attitude perfectly: "If I beat you, I will not ridicule you because, by being my opponent, you made me strive; you made me strong. And without you, I would not be what (and who) I am now. Therefore, I salute you…my opponent!" And so, from an apparent attitude of conflict and competition can come mutual respect, comradeship (for having "gone through it"), and a renewed resolve to improve ourselves whether we lose or win.

The most important element of sports karate is attitude, and the correct attitude to adopt for all competing karate-ka is one of sportsmanship. Competition karate can only be useful if it serves the needs of the group rather than the ego of the individual. In essence, the objectives of sports karate should be: the pursuit of excellence, sportsmanship, teamwork (where appropriate), and the fostering of friendship.

There are two types of karate contests or tournaments: semi-contact and full contact. In semi-contact karate, light, controlled blows are allowed to touch selected targets on an opponent. They must not, however, land with any force or destructive power. To land a blow with real force is to risk injury to both yourself and your opponent. Furthermore, to do so results in disqualification. Full-contact karate requires training similar to kickboxing and boxing. For the purposes of this book, we will focus our attention on semi-contact karate.

These karate-ka embody and can demonstrate the principles of skillful and dignified karate free-sparring. The player on the right skillfully evades a well-executed punch.

REFEREE JUDGING A CONTEST

Dignity, courtesy, and the observance of proper etiquette are vital, even if you lose. This is good karate, even in defeat. Keep dignity, even in defeat. You will most likely get another chance. What profit is there if a man or woman gains the world but loses him- or herself?

THE KARATE CONTEST

The rules for karate contests vary from country to country and from association to association; however, there are a number of standard rules. A center referee, assisted by four corner judges, normally conducts karate contests, and usually there is a chief referee whose decision is final. The karate contest area is 9.5 yards squared (8 meters squared). In the center of this square, two lines

Vic Charles, karate champion, demonstrates the precision in kicking techniques required to be a true champion. All attackers must be aware that executing a kick will, in most cases, leave them open to a retaliatory punch or kick.

FOOT-SWEEP AND TAKEDOWN COMBINATION

STEP 1: Make sure you are relaxed to avoid "telegraphing" (letting your opponent see the foot-sweep coming).

STEP 2: Ensure that you make good firm contact using the sole of your foot.

STEP 3: If necessary, be prepared to "catch" your opponent/training partner to help him or her avoid injury.

are marked 3.3 yards (3 meters) apart. These lines are the fighting marks, and contestants must stay behind their respective marks until the contest begins. A judge sits at each corner of the square with two flags, one red and one white. The flags are there as a signal to the center referee.

One of the contestants wears a red belt, and the other wears a white belt. These belts have nothing to do with the contestant's actual grade or rank, but are merely worn in order to allow a clear distinction to be made between contestants. The belt colors worn relate to the flags carried by the judges, so that points can be awarded depending upon which flag is raised.

CONTEST RULES

The contestant scores a point if he or she delivers an accurate punch, kick, or strike to a recognized target area and with enough perceived power, form, attitude, and control.

A full point is often awarded for the clean delivery of a variety of techniques under the following circumstances:

• When a well-timed attack catches an advancing opponent with a strike.

• An attack delivered to an off-balance opponent.

A FOOT-SWEEP TAKEDOWN AND PUNCH

As your opponent moves towards you, possibly intent on attacking, hook the ankle or calf of his or her forward leg using the sole of your foot. As your opponent topples to the floor, finish up with a controlled punch to his or her midsection or to any proper available target.

- A combination of successive and accurate techniques.
- A takedown (foot-sweep) and punch combination.
- If an opponent loses the will to fight or turns his or her back, a point can be awarded against him or her.
- An attack successfully delivered to an unguarded (but legitimate) target.

Self-defense teachers often claim that the majority of fights will end up in grappling. Karate players must demonstrate a high level of discipline during sparring to ensure this never happens.

ADVANCED KICKING TECHNIQUES

**Flying round kick
(tobi mawashi-geri).**

**Flying front kick
(tobi mae-geri).**

Forbidden techniques and fouls:

• Direct contact attacks to any part of the body except the limbs.

• Direct contact to joints.

• Persistent attacks to the shins to break morale or intimidate.

• Attacks to the eyes or privates.

• Unnecessary or excessive body grabbing and clinching.

• The use of knife-hand or spear-finger strikes.

• Wasting time or leaving the arena too frequently.

• Verbal abuse or provocation.

CONTEST SCORING

• **Ippon** (a full point). The judge raises his or her flag higher than the shoulder.

• **Wazari** (a half point). The judge raises his or her flag lower than the shoulder.

• If the judge sees a foul or thinks a contestant should be disqualified, he or she turns the relevant flag several times above his or her head.

• If the judge sees no score after a clash of contestants, he or she waves both flags right and left, crossing them just above the knees.

• If the judge did not see the clash of techniques at all, he or she momentarily covers both eyes with the flags.

• If the judge is certain that both contestants scored at the same time (known as **Ai-uchi**), he or she points the ends of each flag toward each other in front of the chest.

If no full score has been made at the end of a contest, the referee will call for the judges' decision. The judges will then raise the red or white flag,

Without good control, karate is nothing but an excuse for brutality. Knowing you can win—you can withdraw. To be good at karate is to train for skill. The aim must always be to score points, not to hurt the other player.

depending upon which contestant they think has won. If a judge feels that the contest should be a draw, he or she crosses both flags above the head.

Sometimes, it is assumed that a contestant who might be leading the contest with a half-point score (wazari) will automatically win the contest when time is called. However, this is not necessarily so. If it is felt that the contestant with the lead has been back-pedaling and avoiding his or her opponent in order to cling to the marginal lead, or that he or she has infringed one or more of the rules, he or she will lose the contest. The referee has the power to overrule one judge, but if two or more judges want to award a point, it is usually awarded.

MENTAL PREPARATION

A karate master once asked his students, "Which is more important, the body or the mind?" Some students thought that because the subject was karate, the body—or what it could do—had to be more important. Others thought that the mind was more important. No one realized that the question was a trick. "How can a body do anything without a mind?" the master asked. "And how can a mind do anything without a body? Karate is the fusion of body and mind into one efficient unit!"

Accordingly, just as there is a physical warm-up in karate, there is also a mental warm-up; in the case of a karate contest, there is also an emotional warm-up.

Karate-ka learn to filter out distractions, such as noise, the environment, and all other potential or actual distractions. Any distractions that may affect concentration must be minimized. If interrupted, the karate-ka must learn to return to full power and concentration as quickly as possible.

If you hurry to class for fear of being late, you may arrive on time physically, but not necessarily mentally. Of course, it is always best to be on time; but if you are late, sometimes it is better to slow down, avoid the panic of rushing, and take some time to get focused. This advice is true for anything from a karate tournament to a school examination. This is precisely why part of the karate-ka's mental preparation is to try to avoid

Through dedicated training in the art of karate, the weak can overcome the strong. Here, a junior karate-ka controls the attack of an adult and responds with a devastating counterattack.

tension. Correct (deep) breathing is important, as good oxygenation of the brain is vital for proper concentration.

ADJUSTING TO YOUR ENVIRONMENT

Smells, sights, and sounds filtering in through the senses can cause major distractions if they are not processed and filtered out. For example, say you went to a brand new sports hall to take part in a karate tournament and you lost. The smell of the newly built sports hall might become associated in your mind with failure. Every time you smelled that smell again in the future, you would be at risk of suffering negative feelings and thoughts.

Once your feelings have begun to turn into negative thoughts, you are already becoming handicapped. One way karate-ka (along with sportsmen and -women) deal with such negative thoughts is to perform a ritual of preparation to occupy time and to keep the mind busy. For instance, they might always put their gi top on first or always tie their obi a particular way. Illogical it may be, but in the mental game of emotional preparation, it can count for a lot.

Visualization is another tool that can be used in mental preparation. You might imagine yourself moving strongly and smoothly through your techniques, or you might see yourself winning. Also, assuming you have been training hard and have prepared yourself as well as you can, remember this: do not try too hard, as this can lead to failure. Rely on your body and its natural instincts, for there are some things that the body knows that the mind does not. For instance, your body knows how to fight a cold virus; it knows instinctively how to dodge and duck; and it is packed with a host of defensive reflexes and mechanisms that the thinking mind could never control. So trust your body and let your body and mind work together—you might be surprised at how positive the results are.

YOUR PERSONAL PATH TO KARATE

No matter which path you take to karate and whichever style you choose, remember: although there are many paths, there is only one mountain. Do not forget that you can only travel one path at a time. While you may need to experiment with different methods or styles when you begin, it is always advisable to settle into one, study it hard, and become proficient at it. This does not mean that you cannot branch out or change styles later; it is just that discipline imposed from outside often guards us against our own weaknesses.

Karate demands that we take matters of personal development into our own hands and that we forge the metal of our being in the fire of our will. Put another way, there is no success without sweat, and no sweat without effort; there is no effort without will, and no (effective) will without direction. Karate is a direction, a direction in which to lead your will and make your efforts bear fruit. Karate is more than just self-defense, as we have seen in this book.

Now, as in the past, the efforts made to master the art of karate will yield practical results and will reward those who make them. This is because karate is concerned with life skills and the positive development of the individual, the clan, the province, the nation, and ultimately, the whole of humanity.

Glossary

Ai-uchi	Simultaneous scoring
Bunkai	The practical application of karate
Chi-na	To seize
Chudan	Middle (level)
Dachi	Stance
Do	"Way" (of karate, for example)
Gedan	Lower (level)
Hanmi	Half-facing-appearing stance
Ippon	(One) point/score
Jo	Place
Jodan	Upper (level)
Jutsu	Technique/science/method
karate-do	"The way of karate"
karate-jutsu	"Techniques of karate"
karate-ka	Karate practitioner
Kata	Choreographed sequence of martial arts movements
Koshi o i renu	Putting in the hip
Kumite	Meeting hands; sparring
Maai	Relative distance
Obi	Gi belt
Rei	A curtsy or bow
Sensei	Father or teacher
Tameshiwara	Test or breaking (techniques)

Te	Hand
Tenshin	Body evasion or maneuver
Wazari	A half-point
Zanshin	Awareness, or the remaining mind once distractions are removed
Zenshorindo	A karate style involving pushing-hands, grip escape, and grappling systems

Clothing and Equipment

CLOTHING

Gi: The gi is the most typical martial arts "uniform." Usually in white, but also available in other colors, it consists of a cotton thigh-length jacket and calf-length trousers. Gis come in three weights: light, medium, and heavy. Lightweight gis are cooler than heavyweight gis, but not as strong. The jacket is usually bound at the waist with a belt.

Belt: Belts are used in the martial arts to denote the rank and experience of the wearer. They are made from strong linen or cotton and wrap several times around the body before tying. Beginners usually wear a white belt, and the final belt is almost always black.

Hakama: A long folded skirt with five pleats at the front and one at the back. It is a traditional form of clothing in kendo, iaido, and jujutsu.

Zori: A simple pair of slip-on sandals worn in the dojo when not training to keep the floor clean.

WEAPONS

Bokken: A bokken is a long wooden sword made from Japanese oak. Bokken are roughly the same size and shape as a traditional Japanese sword (katana).

Jo: The jo is a simple wooden staff about 4–5 ft (1.3–1.6 m) long and is a traditional weapon of karate and aikido.

Kamma: Two short-handled sickles used as a fighting tool in some types of karate and jujutsu.

Tanto: A wooden knife used for training purposes.

Hojo jutsu: A long rope with a noose on one end used in jujutsu to restrain attackers.

Sai: Long, thin, and sharp spikes, held like knives and featuring wide, spiked handguards just above the handles.

Tonfa: Short poles featuring side handles, like modern-day police batons.

Katana: A traditional Japanese sword with a slightly curved blade and a single, razor-sharp cutting edge.

Butterfly knives: A pair of knives, each one with a wide blade. They are used mainly in kung fu.

Nunchaku: A flail-like weapon consisting of three short sections of staff connected by chains.

Shinai: A bamboo training sword used in the martial art of kendo.

Iaito: A stainless-steel training sword with a blunt blade used in the sword-based martial art of iaido.

TRAINING AIDS

Mook yan jong: A wooden dummy against which the martial artist practices his blocks and punches and conditions his limbs for combat.

Makiwara: A plank of wood set in the ground used for punching and kicking practice.

Focus pads: Circular pads worn on the hands by one person, while his or her partner uses the pads for training accurate punching.

PROTECTIVE EQUIPMENT

Headguard: A padded, protective helmet that protects the wearer from blows to the face and head.

Joint supports: Tight foam or bandage sleeves that go around elbow, knee, or ankle joints and protect the muscles and joints against damage during training.

Groin protector: A well-padded undergarment for men that protects the testicles and the abdomen from kicks and low punches.

Practice mitts: Lightweight boxing gloves that protect the wearer's hands from damage in sparring, and reduce the risk of cuts being inflicted on the opponent.

Chest protector: A sturdy shield worn by women over the chest to protect the breasts during sparring.

Further Reading

Egami, Shieeru. *The Heart of Karate Do.* Tokyo: Kodansha International, 2000.

Funakoshi, Gichin. *Karate-Do: My Way of Life.* Tokyo: Kodansha International, 1981.

Nakayama, Masatoshi. *Best Karate Series 1-11.* Tokyo: Kodansha International, 1985.

Nakayama, Masatoshi. *Dynamic Karate: Instruction by the Master.* Tokyo: Kodansha International, 1987.

Nishiyama, Hidetaka and Richard C. Brown. *Karate: The Art of Empty-Hand Fighting.* Boston: Charles E. Tuttle Co, 1991.

Rielly, Robin L. *Secrets of Shotokan Karate.* Boston: Charles E. Tuttle Co, 2000.

Sugiyama, Shojiro. *25 Shoto-Kan Kata.* Chicago: Shojiro Sugiyama, 1984.

Wilton, Denis. *The Complete Book of Karatedo.* Marlborough, UK: Crowood Press, 1998.

Useful Web Sites

http://microbiol.org/vl.martial.arts/

http://martialarts.org/

http://www.worldkickboxingassociation.com/

http://www.iskf.com/

http://www.ska.org/

http://www.matsubayashi-ryu.com/

http://www.ikakarate.com/

http://bigbreak.8k.com/corkboard/

About the Author

Nathan Johnson holds a 6th-dan black belt in karate and a 4th-degree black sash in traditional Chinese kung fu. He has studied martial arts for 30 years and holds seminars and lectures on martial arts and related subjects throughout the world. He teaches zen shorindo karate at several leading universities in the U.K. His previous books include *Zen Shaolin Karate* and *Barefoot Zen.* He lives in Hampshire, England.

Index

References in italics refer to illustration captions